SHAI GILGEOUS-ALEXANDER

BASKETBALL SUPERSTAR

BY LUKE HANLON

Book design by Jake Nordby
Cover design by Jake Nordby

Photographs ©: Carlos Osorio/AP Images, cover, 1; Cooper Neill/Getty Images Sport/Getty Images, 4; Kyle Phillips/AP Images, 7; Shutterstock Images, 8; Billy Gates/The Oregonian/AP Images, 11; Andy Lyons/Getty Images Sport/Getty Images, 13, 14; Harry How/Getty Images Sport/Getty Images, 17; Katharine Lotze/Getty Images Sport/Getty Images, 19; Tony Gutierrez/AP Images, 20, 30; Yong Teck Lim/Getty Images Sport/Getty Images, 23; Joshua Gateley/Getty Images Sport/Getty Images, 25; David Zalubowski/AP Images, 26–27; Red Line Editorial, 29

Press Box Books, an imprint of Press Room Editions, Inc.

ISBN
978-1-63494-950-7 (library bound)
978-1-63494-964-4 (paperback)
978-1-63494-991-0 (epub)
978-1-63494-978-1 (hosted ebook)

Library of Congress Control Number: 2024912304

Distributed by North Star Editions, Inc.
2297 Waters Drive
Mendota Heights, MN 55120
www.northstareditions.com

Printed in the United States of America
012025

About the Author
Luke Hanlon is a sportswriter and editor based in Minneapolis. He's written dozens of nonfiction sports books for kids and spends a lot of his free time watching his favorite Minnesota sports teams.

TABLE OF CONTENTS

1 WINNING TIME

The Oklahoma City Thunder had gone cold. They hadn't made a bucket in more than five minutes. All season, the team had relied on Shai Gilgeous-Alexander to score late in games. That strategy didn't change in the playoffs.

The Thunder were playing the New Orleans Pelicans. It was Game 1 in the first round of the 2024 playoffs. New Orleans led 90–88 with less than two minutes to go. That's when Gilgeous-Alexander

Shai Gilgeous-Alexander averaged 27.3 points per game in the first round of the 2024 playoffs.

started to take over. He tied the game with a jump shot. Then the Thunder went back to him. Gilgeous-Alexander drove hard into the paint. A Pelicans defender fouled him. But Gilgeous-Alexander still put up an off-balance shot. The home crowd erupted as the ball hit nothing but net. Then he hit his free throw to put the Thunder up three.

Thunder fans had been waiting for a game like this. Oklahoma City hadn't made the playoffs in four years. And the Thunder hadn't won a playoff series in eight years. Having a star like Gilgeous-Alexander on the

MID-RANGE MASTER

Gilgeous-Alexander's game-tying shot against the Pelicans came from the mid-range. Most teams try to score from the paint or from behind the three-point line. However, Gilgeous-Alexander often finds open shots in the mid-range. During the 2023–24 season, only four players scored more from the mid-range than Gilgeous-Alexander.

Gilgeous-Alexander shoots over Herbert Jones of the New Orleans Pelicans in a 2024 playoff game.

team helped change that. His clutch scoring led Oklahoma City to a 94–92 win in Game 1. Thunder fans couldn't wait to see what their superstar would do next.

2 HOOP DREAMS

Shai Gilgeous-Alexander was born on July 12, 1998. He grew up in Toronto, Ontario. Shai's parents raised him to be competitive. His mom, Charmaine Gilgeous, was a track-and-field athlete. She ran the 400-meter dash in the 1992 Olympics. Shai's father, Vaughn Alexander, taught Shai about basketball. Vaughn started coaching Shai from a young age. He also made sure Shai did his homework.

Shai enjoyed other sports as a kid. He played baseball, football, and soccer.

With a population of more than three million people, Toronto is the largest city in Canada.

Basketball was always his favorite sport, though. Shai dreamed of one day playing in the National Basketball Association (NBA).

When Shai was 11, he and his mom moved to nearby Hamilton, Ontario. At 14, he tried out for his high school basketball team. The coaches didn't think he was good enough to play for the varsity team. So, they put him on junior varsity. Shai was devastated. But Charmaine convinced him to do his best on the junior varsity team.

That turned out to be a good decision. Shai was named the Most Valuable Player (MVP) of the team. He led the team to a city championship, too. After that season, Shai transferred to a different high school. He made the varsity team. And he had even more success. Before his junior year, Shai thought

In 2017, Shai Gilgeous-Alexander (4) played in a game alongside the top high school players from around the world.

he needed to face tougher competition. So, he moved away from his family to Chattanooga, Tennessee.

Shai spent two years at Hamilton Heights Christian Academy. Scouts loved his quickness and his vision. Shai almost always found open teammates. He could also blow past defenders to score at the rim. During his junior year, Shai committed to the University of Florida.

In the summer of 2016, Shai took part in a basketball camp. College coaches thought his skills had greatly improved. Now, several top schools wanted Shai. In November 2016, he changed his mind. Shai decided to play at the University of Kentucky instead of Florida. Kentucky was known for producing top NBA players.

Kentucky's head coach, John Calipari, didn't lie to Shai. All of Kentucky's starters had committed

CANADIAN CONNECTION

While growing up in Ontario, Shai Gilgeous-Alexander played against Jamal Murray. Murray went on to star at Kentucky during the 2015–16 season. The Denver Nuggets then drafted Murray in 2016. Shai said he watched almost every game Murray played for Kentucky.

ESPN ranked Shai Gilgeous-Alexander as the 35th best high school player in his class before he committed to Kentucky.

before Shai had. So, he would have to work hard for a starting spot. That wasn't going to be a problem. Nothing was going to stop him from realizing his childhood dream.

3 TRADING PLACES

Shai Gilgeous-Alexander went to Kentucky determined to be great. He always arrived at the practice gym earlier than his teammates. Off the court, he studied hard and earned good grades. His work ethic stood out to the Kentucky coaches. However, he didn't start games. He came off the bench in 13 of his first 15 games for the Wildcats.

By January, things had changed. Gilgeous-Alexander became a regular starter. He developed into Kentucky's best

Gilgeous-Alexander averaged 14.4 points per game during his freshman year at Kentucky.

player. Gilgeous-Alexander led the Wildcats to the championship game of the Southeastern Conference (SEC) Tournament. They faced the University of Tennessee. The Volunteers had already beaten Kentucky twice during the 2017–18 season. Gilgeous-Alexander made sure the Wildcats wouldn't lose again. He scored 29 points to win the SEC title.

Gilgeous-Alexander impressed NBA teams while he played at Kentucky. After the season, Gilgeous-Alexander decided to go pro. The Charlotte Hornets selected him with the 11th pick in the 2018 NBA Draft. On the night of the draft, the Hornets traded Gilgeous-Alexander to the Los Angeles Clippers.

Gilgeous-Alexander came off the bench in his NBA debut. The rookie made five of his six shots and scored 11 points. He quickly adapted

to the speed of the NBA. The Clippers coaches couldn't keep him on the bench for long. Gilgeous-Alexander started his first NBA game three weeks later. He never went back to the bench after that. After the season, he earned a spot on the NBA All-Rookie Second Team. The Clippers seemed to have a future star. However, the Clippers traded for superstar Paul George in the summer of 2019. In return, the Oklahoma City Thunder asked for Gilgeous-Alexander as part of the deal.

Gilgeous-Alexander didn't like being traded. But there was a bright side. Oklahoma City had recently traded for veteran point guard Chris Paul. Gilgeous-Alexander had often watched Paul to improve his own skills as a point guard. Now, he got to play with him.

Experts didn't expect the Thunder to win many games ahead of the 2019–20 season. Gilgeous-Alexander helped Oklahoma City surprise the NBA. He led the

FAMILY TIES

Shai Gilgeous-Alexander grew up playing basketball against his cousin Nickeil Alexander-Walker. They each dreamed of playing against each other in the NBA. On November 2, 2019, that dream became a reality. The cousins guarded each other whenever they were both in the game. The Thunder beat Alexander-Walker's New Orleans Pelicans 115–104.

Gilgeous-Alexander averaged 3.3 assists per game in his first season with the Thunder.

team with 19 points per game. Better yet, the Thunder made the playoffs. They lost in the first round. But their future looked promising with Gilgeous-Alexander leading the way.

4 MAKING THE LEAP

The Thunder traded Chris Paul after the 2020–21 season. The team trusted Shai Gilgeous-Alexander to be a leader. However, injuries forced him to miss 61 games over the next two seasons.

Gilgeous-Alexander entered the 2022–23 season fully healthy. Nearly all of his scoring stats increased. Most point guards prefer to stay out of the paint. But Gilgeous-Alexander constantly attacked the basket. Defenders struggled to guard him without fouling. And when he got to

Gilgeous-Alexander made 51 percent of his shots during the 2022–23 season.

the free-throw line, Gilgeous-Alexander rarely missed. He averaged a career-high 31.4 points per game. His performance earned him a spot on the All-NBA First Team. Gilgeous-Alexander had become one of the league's best players.

Gilgeous-Alexander didn't take much time off after the season. In August 2023, he suited up for Canada in the Basketball World Cup. Gilgeous-Alexander led Canada in scoring. The Canadians made a run to the bronze-medal game. They faced the United States. The Americans had come into the tournament as favorites. Gilgeous-Alexander wasn't fazed. He controlled the Canadian offense with 31 points and 12 assists. His play led Canada to an upset win and a bronze medal.

Going into the 2023–24 season, Oklahoma City had a young roster. Now 25 years old,

Gilgeous-Alexander averaged 26.3 points per game in the 2023 Basketball World Cup.

Gilgeous-Alexander was the veteran leader of the team. He continued to score with ease. When defenders hounded him, he set up his teammates to score. Gilgeous-Alexander once again made the All-NBA First Team. He also finished second in voting for the MVP Award.

Gilgeous-Alexander led his young team to new heights. The Thunder won 57 games. They hadn't won that many games in 10 years. More importantly, they earned the best record in the Western Conference.

In the playoffs, Gilgeous-Alexander raised his game. The Thunder faced the New Orleans Pelicans in the first round. Gilgeous-Alexander scored the most points in each game of the series. He helped the Thunder sweep New Orleans.

Oklahoma City then faced the Dallas Mavericks. Many fans consider Mavs superstar Luka Dončić one of the league's best players.

FASHION ICON

Basketball isn't Shai Gilgeous-Alexander's only passion in life. He also loves fashion. Before games, he often wears stylish outfits to the arena. Men's fashion magazine *GQ* took notice. The magazine named Gilgeous-Alexander the most stylish NBA player in 2022 and 2023.

Gilgeous-Alexander scored the most points for the Thunder in all 10 of their playoff games in 2024.

But Gilgeous-Alexander was often the best player on the court. His teammates struggled to make shots, though. The Mavericks won the series in six games.

The Thunder's season ended in disappointment. Even so, Gilgeous-Alexander continued to improve. The future looked bright for Oklahoma City.

CLUTCH SHOT

In a December 2023 game, the Thunder trailed the Denver Nuggets by one point with nine seconds left. Shai Gilgeous-Alexander drove hard into the paint. Then he took a turnaround jump shot. The ball went through the hoop with 0.9 seconds left. The win helped the Thunder earn the top spot in the Western Conference.

TIMELINE

1. Toronto, Canada (July 12, 1998)
Shai Gilgeous-Alexander is born.

2. St. Louis, Missouri (March 11, 2018)
Gilgeous-Alexander scores 29 points and leads Kentucky to the SEC Tournament Championship.

3. Brooklyn, New York (June 21, 2018)
The Charlotte Hornets select Gilgeous-Alexander with the 11th pick in the NBA Draft. The Hornets then trade him to the Los Angeles Clippers.

4. Los Angeles, California (October 17, 2018)
In his NBA debut, Gilgeous-Alexander scores 11 points.

5. Oklahoma City, Oklahoma (December 23, 2022)
Gilgeous-Alexander scores a career-high 44 points against the New Orleans Pelicans.

6. Salt Lake City, Utah (February 19, 2023)
Gilgeous-Alexander plays in his first NBA All-Star Game.

7. Manila, Philippines (September 10, 2023)
Gilgeous-Alexander records 31 points and 12 assists to help Canada win bronze at the 2023 Basketball World Cup.

8. New Orleans, Louisiana (April 29, 2024)
Gilgeous-Alexander leads the Thunder to a four-game sweep against the Pelicans.

MAP

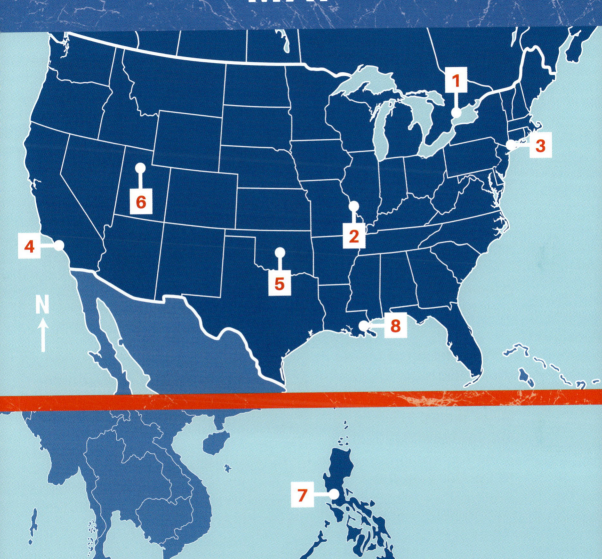

AT A GLANCE

Birth date: July 12, 1998

Birthplace: Toronto, Ontario

Position: Point guard

Shoots: Right

Size: 6-foot-6 (198 cm), 180 pounds (82 kg)

Current team: Oklahoma City Thunder (2019–)

Previous team: Los Angeles Clippers (2018–19)

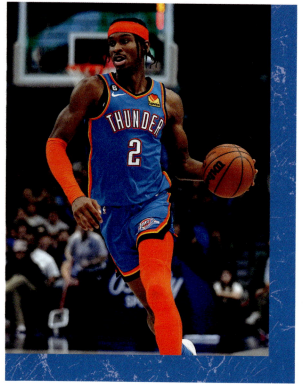

Major awards:
SEC Tournament MVP (2018),
All-Rookie Second Team (2019), All-NBA First Team (2023, 2024),
All-Star (2023, 2024)

Accurate through the 2023–24 season.

GLOSSARY

clutch
Successful in a difficult situation when the outcome of the game is in question.

conference
A smaller group of teams that make up part of a sports league.

debut
First appearance.

mid-range
The area of the court inside the three-point line and outside of the paint.

paint
Another term for the lane, the area between the basket and the free-throw line.

rookie
A first-year player.

sweep
When a team wins all the games in a series.

upset
An unexpected victory by a supposedly weaker team or player.

veteran
A player who has spent several years in a league.

vision
The ability to see how a play is developing and to know what will happen next.

TO LEARN MORE

Books

Giedd, Steph. *Oklahoma City Thunder*. Mendota Heights, MN: Press Box Books, 2024.

Hanlon, Luke. *Everything Basketball*. Minneapolis: Abdo Publishing, 2024.

James, Ryan. *Top NBA Finals*. Coral Springs, FL: Seahorse Publishing, 2022.

More Information

To learn more about Shai Gilgeous-Alexander, go to **pressboxbooks.com/AllAccess.**

These links are routinely monitored and updated to provide the most current information available.

INDEX